Twenty Twenty:

Treatments for Cut Flowers

Arthur Allen

erbacce-press
Liverpool UK

Acknowledgements:

Acknowledgements and thanks are due to the editors of erbacce-press for realising this book.

Air Canada Canto was chosen as a finalist in the Malahat Review Open Season Awards 2021.

She Sleeps was shortlisted for the Jane Martin Poetry Prize 2021.

for my mother & grandmother

A man who knows neither how to travel nor how
to keep a journal has put together this travel journal.
But at the moment of signing he is suddenly afraid.
So he casts the first stone. Here.

Henri Michaux
Ecuador

Contents:

A Picture of Loss in a Fruitless Year

I do not mean to tell this story
as if it is the only one.

In the fragile skin
of an overripe tomato
I remember your cheek.

'Is My Nan Going to Die?', CBBC

To alleviate the pandemic anxieties of children
kids' TV is hastily responding to coronavirus,
but it's hardly Mr Rodgers explaining:
'What does assassination?' mean
after the death of Bobby Kennedy.

Children have very deep feelings,
he said, just the way parents do,
just the way everybody does

and his plea was simply: do not leave them
to the mercy of their own
fantasies of loss,

but strive to understand
and find their feelings with curiosity
like little books you haven't read.

•

I wrote in my notebook -
How do we nurture new attitudes to death?
     and then my gran began to die
     so gently I barely knew
     I was stepping off
     the crest of her life.

W
(1932 – 2020)

I.

I possess a great love secretly
for one name inside me

so great and so secret
I write it this way : W

II.

The word of your name
has become too tender to speak

since it was spoken commandingly
somewhere final and only

by delivering the life of every particle
of you towards the call could it be answered,

each minuscule grain constituting its degree of aching.
According to the order of time

you had no choice
but to make yourself alone.

III.

Where - with nothing
exterior left of you

should I set down
your crowning character

in which you have been a guest

only

and to what
does it now refer?

DNR Order, Still Life

Even if you do not recall
the talk with the doctor
it is still your destiny,
 but W-
do not look at it.

Do not compel yourself to know
what is lying on the hall table; it is there
solely, crucially, for the instruction of others.

An instruction to inaction.
A shard of paper
among papers on the table.

Your fate suspended on the table
like Aslan (I think in brighter moods) or
something set mid-aspic (in the gloom).

The unspeakable passes,
barely spoken, over the land:
already it's noon.
                              Ingeborg Bachmann

Natural vs Sudden Death

I.

All spring
 death strikes
  where it wants

like something effortless
and without human delay
transmitted into effect

 the edict: die
and across the world
 it was obeyed.

II.

A certain jannock pace
used to wave in the happening

of things like planting after winter
and harvesting in fall

but an older darker rhythm
is master of this year.

It is parents and grandparents who are dying.
It is children who remain
and no longer are quite children.

This year is the season
when all friends may and do die daily.

Days drop off
like worried scabs.

III.

The meaning
  of natural death

different, somehow,
  from sudden death

though both arrive
  at their own appointed time
 and at no other,

  ordained by biology
death by the plan of us
  not death by our designs.

Death by anatomical destiny
    is shocking, is sudden only
      to us who must record it.

Surely the lives of the old
are briefer than the young
          Robert Lowell

Childhood is long
and narrow like a coffin,
  and you can't get out of it on your own.
            Tove Ditlevsen

•

Strange hands have succeeded her own,
they hide pain poorly,
they do not recall secretarial school:
her handwriting has dissolved
into something childlike
from a childhood not her own, they fix
someone else's white hair: this she finds
drifting everywhere.

     On entering the hospice
she quickly laid her phone down
and did not lift it up again.

Leaning her life
against the strength of another
as though riding pillion
maybe relieved the pain a little.

     In Ontario
     I carry my grandmother
          under my heart.

THIRST

*This gives one an idea of consumption: [DRAWING]
in the middle a faceted stone, at the side the saws,
otherwise everything empty, dry sputum.*

*A little water; these bits of pills stick in the mucus like
splinters of glass.*

Everything, even the beer, burned me.

*Tell me again how your mother drank, only water, long-
lasting pain, thirst.*

*I cannot drink a single glass of water, though the craving
itself is some satisfaction.*

A lake doesn't flow into anything, you know.

*Ask whether there is good mineral water, just out of
curiosity.*

*How wonderful that is, isn't it? The lilac –
dying, it drinks, goes on swilling. That cannot be,
that a dying man drinks.*

*Somewhere in today's newspaper there is an excellent little
item on the treatment of cut flowers; they're so terribly
thirsty ... so they can drink more; strip their leaves.*

(Kafka, *Conversation Slips*)

She Sleeps

and does not reach for my mother's hands,
she sleeps with her hands in an attitude of prayer
between her thighs: her place of comfort - just below
her mortal wound - drawn up legs an abatis
against the enemy within her colon,
against the throes of it, against the caiman-like uncurling.

(The law of nettles:
where the damage breeds,
there too grows the green-leafed cure.)

This is how she slept at the end
and this is how she sleeps
into her ending life.

Her hands, so thin even held together.

Sleep without before or after.
Sleep that goes beyond
past, present, or future.

(A drawing by Durer of the hands of an apostle
forces itself upon my attention as at no other time.
                    I don't even like it.)

What was she?
Two closed eyes: the sum of all that had been.
                    Violette Leduc

Just Rest

At this point
it is worse

when she tries to speak
than when she stays sleeping.

What kindled her
is being quenched

she is
no longer

rising or setting
but a part of the vanishing

sensitive voiceless species
of the dying,

Kafka is included here:
49 kilos in his winter clothes.

W- Is No Longer Speaking

The natural state of her eyes
is closed.

Let them be closed,
this night is prelude only.

Closed may be the natural state of all eyes.
Her body is a cooling crucible for soundless sleep.

Lie here now
as though this were
where you lay
every evening of your life.

It is nearly time to take your brushes
take your pen and disappear.

Wrote, stopped, tears.

Yesterday evening a late bee drank the white lilac dry.
Kafka, *Conversation Slips*

Dear N-, I'm Sure

you are doing good talking and touching of skin,
and you were right to fight to keep the iron out
of her blood where it would only have kicked
and started like a steam hammer or a horse in miniature,

energising her briefly for no nameable purpose
but prolonging, and (all this against her wishes),
would have forced her eyes to open on an extant future
she is indivisibly within already.

There is nought to manage
but this state, which is beyond her,

she knows now that she herself
is to be the sacramental thing
and so is already holy

the past glowing in her, the future poured out,
her body inaudibly emptying of history.
Her bed is a vehicle afloat and passing
at an even pace that does not disturb the birds.

Her view from the barge is brickwork
moving overhead and less and less
veined with sunlight. She is profoundly separate
from her daughter at the tiller, she drifts

abed upon the river. Death
always was a passage over water.

Her Words

I.

Gallons and gallons
of crushed strawberries and creamed
corn is flowing into the nursing home.
Soft copious rivers of congee flood
past the sagely nodding relicts.

My grandmother says:
I don't know where my words have gone.

II.

A virtuoso talker, and she *liked* to talk:
serine in tessitura, and in volume an undergrowth
of softness. Speech that should be heard
inside of gardens. Laughter: a silver jangling of bangles
                              and little bells,
the kind that bring faithful animals in from the hillside.
But to recall her speaking is not easy, and tomorrow
is not easier.

III.

I dream her words
all wilder
and submerge
in seething pastel waves.

The birds
of her laugh
leave their tiny islands

eroded by wind
they are slipping under,
in the Sea of Okhotsk

they disappear
without much noticing

 – a wrist
and some ankles
perceived a pull and clutch
sing down the wave-line
in the instant after.

The silence is like a fine spiderweb against my face,
I cannot rub it off, it is simply there
without being tangibly real.
                    Artur Lundkvist

CONVALESENCE

Can the pain temporarily stop? I mean, for a fairly long time.

*Even if there should be scarification – forgive all this
disgusting questioning, but you are my doctor, aren't you?*

So the help goes away again without helping.

*They killed the man beside me, every assistant doctor
dropped in and without asking.*

*How many years will you be able to stand it? How long will
I be able to stand your standing it?*

*It's obvious the way one devilish medicine smooths the way
for the next.*

Let the bad remain bad, otherwise it will grow worse.

(Kafka, *Conversation Slips*)

Death Arrives

I.

Still locked down in Ontario.
No one is answering their phone.
This can only mean W- has died.

One thought all day,
but it is projection only. W- silently
lives on, meaning: she continues to die.

A text from my mum in the late afternoon:

Just got home.
There was a program about Ceylon on TV
so left mum with that on and told a nurse
I was going and to please keep an eye on her for me.

Sometimes we must walk away from death
because it is time for us to go home,

though death may be close enough to throw
tall shadows on the screen door.

II.

My friend Pat is in the garden suddenly.
The day W- seemed to die has changed.
Pat's cat, Blackie, has died.

Pat comes inside without saying any words,
there is rabbit-like trembling in his eyes.
They caught one of us today, say his eyes,
and it was the one who ran beside me
for fifteen years, and when he was tired
I carried him like the harvest over my shoulder
and we ran on through the hounding world.

The house was garlanded with crows
but no one saw this coming.

The gift of weeping
is passed round the table.

Pat opens his mouth slowly as though a little bird
is quivering behind his teeth in fright at the suddenness
of sound and sunlight. He still says nothing.

Almost in a whisper his partner tells us what happened,
and Pat sits, wiping his face with the dignity of one man
who can't stop thinking: I must have finished weeping.

Right in the heart of the thought, he weeps.
And holds his head in both hands like a teapot
that has broken into three pieces
and must be held together tightly.

There is a sense in the room that I have buried pets
before and will know the right officiations in an English
way. This is partially true, but I fear my accent has
spoken for me too knowingly. They believe me to be an
authority on the burial rites of small animals. I gently
say, we'll bury him. The service will be tomorrow.

Fear again and again.
Every limb as tired as a person.
Put your hand on my forehead just a moment to give me courage.
                    Kafka, *Conversation Slips*

Bells

After a spell of digging the spade begins to ring
at every meeting with the earth,
and soon my shoulder starts to sound

plangent. There is a scene in Hamlet: enter
two Clowns *[with spades and pickaxes]*.

3ft for a cat. It was maybe 2 1/2
when I stopped, and my sister-in-law
stopped beside me and we sweated
quietly and the world rang out into silence.

If colours are the deeds of light,
its deeds and sufferings
and colour itself
a degree of darkness

how can I see at all
this black cat, coiled
at the distant foot
of our earthwork?

I begin to read a Rilke poem.
Not a long one (not Orpheus)
a cat one, and the bloodbells
chime in the chests of crows.

In the house of the dead
swing many cradles.

Obsequies for Blackie

The body is in a cardboard box outside.
Inside the box is the body, and inside
the body is the cat. Truffle black
a folded length of Van Gogh's crows.

Neatly hidden by the box
is a stillness

wherein all the looks that ever
fell inside of him are vanishing.

The box like a stone
paving the grave
- two feet of empty air.

*These crows he painted two days before he died with the gunshot
that killed him in his belly cramming a canvas with black crows and
beneath them a kind of field, livid perhaps, but empty in any case,
where the red wine colour of the earth clashes frantically with the
dirty yellow wheat. Van Gogh released his crows a few centimetres
from the top and as if from the bottom of the canvas.*

Antonin Artaud

*The crows maintain that a single crow could destroy the heavens.
There is no doubt about that, but it proves nothing against the
heavens, for heaven means simply: the impossibility of crows.*

Kafka, *Wedding in the Country*

Vanishing Upon Vanishing

I.

When she got home from the hospice
my mother discovered all the recordings
had disappeared from her TV.
She could have done without that, and
it distressed me beyond words
that everything could be so absolutely faithless,
so prone to disappearing. I slept
desperately with crossed fingers and crossed
twigs of rowan for their returning
by the same magic as took them away.

W- died early in the morning.

II.

My arms ache from digging the cats grave.
The hospice can't keep W- for more than 24hrs
- their mortuary is uniquely small.
Pure anger like a beautiful red sunset.

III.

Blackie lay in the grave
like a flute in a box.

Pat cried and closed the earth
like a velvet lid.

•

I was not there and did not stay to watch you leave her

                               to Ceylon, to Kandy,
to grow feathers long enough to wrap up well
and go wandering warmly in the infant groves

she keeps inside her – a sleeping dust
blown way of cobra saffron, the Dutch Burgher days:
nine in the family, plus an ox
and cats under the palm shade.

Flit of leopards past the firelight
like ships on the shifting edge
of the navigable seas. They sleep
encircling weapons and embers.

W- walks between them cloaked in feathers
of grebe and eider. Rid the ballast of organs
she goes lightly, at her feet her childhood
sleeps in its *chapelle ardent* of mango leaves
and a programme about Ceylon

did bring her to morning. And now she will live
a little way into this one morning.

•

Before she went into the hospice
she said: *you need to know*
　　what I'm thinking
　because I can't say it any longer
and, of course, N- knew.

But how could they say she was comfortable
when they couldn't save her mouth from drought.

It took almost two days – bloodlessness,
struggling to swallow, a torrid build up

blocking her mouth like a healing well
abandoned and choked up with yellow iris.

"I wonder what it looks like inside?" I asked the nurse.
"Like the witch's kitchen," she said honestly.
Kafka, *postcard on the state of his larynx.*
　　　Sanatorium Wiener Wald. April 13. 1924

Cut flowers should be treated quite differently.
　　　Kafka, *Conversation Slips*

•

She opened her eyes. N- held her face.
She tried twice to say something. N- said: *don't,*
don't waste your energy trying to keep your eyes open.
W- shook her head and her eyes stayed open
and it was known that she meant: *it's not a waste*
of energy to stay and look at you, my only daughter.

•

I was not there and did not stay to see you

let out your breath
like a plait unravelling
in the soft den of your chest

overwintered
  your last breath
        emerged
gentle as a caterpillar
you had sheltered for so long.

For N- as her mother dies

My mum suffers bad dreams:
dreams of distrust in hospital settings,
powerless before wrongness, too much
to relate – no sense of safekeeping.

My mum tells me almost accidentally:
she doesn't know any numbers by heart
except her mums which is useless now
and not even connected.

I want to tell her; go
with your dog and the dogs of our history,
walk in areas of outstanding natural beauty
where to think is no longer to exhaust oneself,
where the sunshine and the swallows
do your thinking as you.

Air Canada Canto

I.

An old woman from Edmonton explained to me on the plane
that after her mother died, she learned you can cry
while doing anything: swimming, cooking, leaving.

When she took off
her dark wool cap
a blue plastic dental-hygiene tool appeared
and started singing like a thrush in her hair,
blue body buried in a tight white nest

  it sang Jerusalem
      over the Atlantic coast

until I asked her if I could take it out
and then she laughed and made me swear
I wouldn't tell my family and it sat on the tray-table
comfortably, looking a little lost now, no longer singing
but lit by sunlight that had never passed through clouds.

II.

Her mother
was a bargain hunter
diagnosed with cervical cancer
in the seventies. She sat on the shore
of Lake Ontario with two gloves
newly bought and fluttering in her lap,
suddenly unsure if she would ever wear them out

wondering what a bargain was
now time was something else
and what was useful
and what would last.

No longer with the burden of safekeeping
        (now it was her who would not last)
    she sat on the sand like a severed hand
  watching sandpipers
    running up to the waves.

Sometimes I cry this way:
like *someone other than myself was weeping in me,*
        particularly midair.

Terminus, God of Boundaries

(Edinburgh from Toronto via Amsterdam)

I.

I do not know where I am
coming from, or going, nor who is travelling.

The airport draws out a dance
in which the loneliness of every character is expressed.

Thinking of my father, dead four years,
and W- now joining him outside the world.

It was only too recently I discovered:
he was mortal and willing to leave me.

I'm still here. And it goes on
 - *the fat, prosperous breeding
of mediocre folks*. Abominate them.

I apologise.

It is only your bliss,
health and comfort
that angers me. Nothing
that is *personally* yours.

II.

Edinburgh is shaggy and unfamiliar with early summer.
I lose sight of the path in high grass.

So many weeds
blooming and seeding
and dying at any time.

Under a bomber's moon I can see clearly
that I don't know where I am.

It's very strange to start off
somewhere
and finish up
    so far from there
        (though it is to be expected).

•

Outside your flat
my mum tells the dog
– there's no one inside.

No matter how slight, it is a scene from history.
David Berman

Her Things

Here is the heart of the sadness: every object
and all that remains half finished - the evidence
of a life in motion now must be expunged.
They are too clearly the face of the fact of her loss,
a single shock felt again and again: she was
                        and now is never
going to finish the shampoo and conditioner
which stand impudently upright and brightly
coloured in the showers corners like attendant
figures in a painting. They are the principle disciples
washing the feet of her absence. She used to step
here naked and bravely dry her body round
the stoma bag in her old-fashioned, olive-coloured
bathroom. The saddest things of all:
                        those that have been saved
for a special day which will no longer arrive.

> How dumb and strangely secretive they are!
> Past our oblivion they will live on,
> familiar blind, not knowing we have gone.
> *Jorge Luis Borges*

FLOWERS

*Show me the columbine; too bright to stand with the
others. Scarlet hawthorn is too hidden, too much in the
dark. And move the lilacs into the sun.*

*Do you have a moment?
Then please lightly spray the peonies.*

*Please see the peonies don't touch the bottom of the
vase. That's why they must be kept in bowls.
Doesn't the newspaper say: Greenish translucent bowls?*

*I'd especially like to take care of the peonies
because they are so fragile.*

*We'll buy a little book about these matters; one has to
know such things precisely.*

See the lilacs, fresher than morning.

*I wanted to wait on the road for her wagon to pass and
give her flowers, but delayed too long with the gardener,
missed the wagon, and can now decorate my room with
flowers.*
            Kafka, *picture postcard (Rumburk),
            to Felix Weltsch. Fall 1918*

But now enough flowers for the time being.

(Kafka, *Conversation Slips*)

Pegasus, Objet Trouvé

Pegasus, in soapstone much repaired:
glued mid-remiges and at the neck,
all four legs missing, but still winged.

She loved it so much
when one leg broke
(to forestall further tragedy)
she had all the other legs cut off.

(I, too, have hobbled far
past hope and fear like a legless horse
 - too dumb for despairing, but no longer carrying
like a stunned bird the hope of wholeness, or resurrection.)

The triumph of this Pegasus
 - outside his proud tossing head
 and mane - the wings: smaller
than his muscular neck which arches down
so snout and foretop touch to chest but powerful
enough to lift a stallion towards heaven.

His wings jut from the flanks
and show (soft in the soapstone) long flight feathers
described by gentle pleats. Four locks of mane
race down his back like braided waves.

Wherever you set
the legless horse down
he is emerging through cloud.

•

I know two things:

W- was picking hawthorn in the lane
to dress her mother's Blackheath bedroom

with the Suffolk autumn
when she heard that she had died.

N- was folding and ironing W-'s undershirts
when the phone told her that she had died.

Are some laws still in place then?

The Coach House

The patient garden listens
to the dead dog breaking down
like fire working underground.

Whatever happens here
began in the past.

We have forsaken the house
where G- could almost be still
looking out the front window

forsaken the wild
spiders that live indoors
and move like wind without direction

forsaken the knothole
in the oblong table
where my fingers hid
all crumbs away.

Left to its own heraldic devices,
the house was purely
then it was developed:
hideous and huge,
vanity without beauty.

I pad past on stockinged feet
seeking the grave of a dog
beyond the strandline of houselights,

our dog – unhonoured, unnoticed
under earth as he is forbidden
(forbid in) heaven.

Simple grammarye in the upturned grounds:
how to unbar the door
for one who does not knock.

Notice as a lance of homesickness
the pond where the snake was seen
is gone entirely. Leaving

only Bonzo, our Border terrier:
revived for months by lemon drizzle cake
went on to die from vital organ deceleration

while I was in East Anglia, and my twin
in Cambridge; his room an octagon
fitting only a circular rug in the centre
that shed its coir before the horrified bedder.

The garden cauldron
fills with blood-coloured smoke.
Magic is ending, the magic of thoughts
fenced for eighty-seven years.

This place is death's fortress
      and so am I.

At the end

of the first day in the hospice, which two weeks later she
would never leave, no one had unpacked the little
suitcase my grandmother brought with her, and maybe
she didn't even know that it remained unopened and, in
that way, did it really matter, but if my mum hadn't
arrived and opened it and folded all her things away, one
can't know when it would have opened. No sense of
holiday. My heart. My mother's heart. My
grandmother's closed eyes. Two weeks after the funeral,
neutralizing her space in Bromley, the case stays closed;
my mum can't open it, can't unpack it now. And I
wouldn't' know how to. She packed it for the first time
then unpacked it and packed it again and for the length
of the moment this little case stays closed, cloistering the
useless clothes, unfinished creams, and slippers, while,
outside the case, her whole flat is deliberately
transformed no longer to include her.

*"As I said to someone –
my bikini days are over
but I have had them,"*
says my grandmother
impossibly quietly
and in the past.

•

The terrier bleakened
as we wend away
unbalanced by dregs
of oils and imperishable foods
from cupboards freshly shorn where all the spices
that expired in early 2000 smell of one great spice
that strongly, hiddenly, has been inventing itself:
a microbic experiment we've ended
in the chemist's absence.
Of her possessions
nothing will be left in cobwebs or in mystery.

   Already cavernous
        the emptiness within
                spills out after us, and
                        sets to harrowing the stairwell.

●

Do you promise
that after a silence
we all learn to bear

they all come back:
the grandmothers, old dogs and fathers?

A bird was in the room
(Kafka, *Conversation Slips*)

•

Read my distant uncles' eulogy with half an eye
the other eye (and a half) was watching
water fall below the overbrimming sweetpea.
The flower joined the flagstones by a quiet cataract.

•

Last Christmas, this house, wrote this
short note consisting of 1) poetical title
and 2) the voice of my mother:

The body of spoken prophecy extends over W-   1)

I knitted her a bobble hat for Christmas   2)
but I don't know
if she'll ever leave the house again

Note below it:

The Pink Rascal and the Lemon Star
   Amaryllis bulbs,
twin globes of hugely varying size

- in consternation, N- holds them up
to the kitchen light like a simple solar system.
If she takes her hands away, they may just hang there
floating bodies.

Burt the Beagle got into the recycling

Stringy paper confetti dressed the garden, too much of it
carrying the name: ---, (which I write W-), who kept so
many envelopes to somehow use again, all of which my
mum encounters alongside precious and unprecious
things as she slowly clears the flat.

She dissolves most documents she meets like rice
paper dissolves in running water (the water must be
imagined moving between her hands) using a shredder,
but now all that was tediously shredded over breakfast
embroiders the dark lawn. Burt the beagle scattered what
was mechanically separated and composed it in a
fluttering sea, marcelling the grass with one name.

My mother and her friend, Burt's steward, follow
the wild dance of the dog over the lawn and into the
pond to gather them back, an indignity that could have

brought tears. The trumpet of the beagle; between a
foghorn and a soul in torment, triumphantly cantering
between long white ribbons. Despite the box of Boneo
biscuits that drove him grabbling through the guts of the
bin having been found empty, he was in good spirits. I
think he just enjoys an atmosphere of movement.

The energy of the morning; sparrows and
daffodils in the window, sill furbelowed with cards, good
dog under the bench, coffee in a mug that touches her
heart, the feeding in by twos and threes (the shredder
was W-'s, and suffers from a low maximum capacity),
the emptying out, the slow and savage teeth, and some
envelopes could just folded up and fitted neatly into the
recycling.

They gather the fragments of her mother's name
filling their arms like children under fruit trees.

•

There's always some distance between us
when N- returns from walking the dog
suspicious that I've been smoking

in her absence, and of course I have been
which lends an ominous feeling
to our first re-joining contact

on the bench with good air flow
between us and my face and my lips
wrapped protectively in scented moisturiser

wasps round our shoulders are audibly whittling
the wood-rind of the bench in their small jaws
and carrying it away, the disconnected pulp is
somewhere becoming nest.

Silver birch seeds fall without end
and sparrows are in the arbour.

Tomorrow is the funeral.

•

The last four years were a surprise and a mess,
now you're going to your mother's funeral
in a sea green dress but you did wonderful work
on the service sheet; on the front it's the 50's
and Wendy at twenty, black and white, a social club
beauty still safekeeping the emerald ring that she sold in
Toronto for something to live on - and on the back-page
she's smiling and looking out, brilliant as I remember her
(already old) - in the middle, instead of your dad, a
single photograph of the orchid he gave you that lasted
for years reads like a poem on its own - forking purple
and white and deeply symbolic. N- you've done a
wonderful job on the service sheet.

                    (But don't all officiate of funerals
have the strangest names - what would I like them to
have? Something biblical or antiquated, I doubt it - but
all their names are robustly their own – most memorably:
David Commander, who presided sturdily over
my father's ceremony, and now for the suddenly
peaceful Sri Lankan princess - Debbie DeVito -
no relation to Danny, outside alliteration.)

The Mother is she who makes all things possible
(even when those things seem to be done against her;
*   even when at least some of those things must necessarily*
*   have been done against what she stood for).*
                                                    B.S. Johnson

•

Sweet road
leading to a sweet building
- it is a crematorium,
dressed in red green Virginia creeper.

I Entered

      roughly following
the stage directions for Ophelia
– long hair down (as outer garb
 of madness) and distributing

flowers of memory, that is – rosemary,
which my mother sometimes forgets
to bring to a bench among fir trees
that is my father's grave approximate.

The spot is no spot – it is a place because he died
and there the steepness of the climb gives out.
He has heard nothing from me for so long
he may think I am dead.

The root-bed never ceases to support him.
The herb is to be threaded through a knothole.
Annually the treetops fill with starlings
as if commanded by a book on Death.

I think Ophelia plays a lute. I did not,
but nonetheless came visibly raving.

The two-metre expanse
between me and anyone
felt like my doing.

> *there she goes*
> *Darkfish, finger to her lips,*
> *Staringly into the afterworld.*
> Ted Hughes

After the Service

milling about
there in the theatre of many-peopled grief,
the flat devoid but populous, and G-
who should have been there but of course is dead,
must be intercostal between my twin and myself.
Us both smiling steadily like sad toys.

In moments of stress
we both sigh, few other signs of tension.
Before our driving test we both sighed,
and the instructor said, you must be brothers.
I can hear him beside me, breathing out heavily,
as we endure the living room.

HG Wells - whose father
was an *ingenious fast bowler*
(if you think such things are genius)
grew up sickly and poor and smart in Bromley
which he described as a "suburb of the damnedest".

My grandmother lived here for the last twenty years.
From the high window of her flat, I watch our outer
family flee like leverets.
They do not like it amid damnation.

At the butcher's this morning - the last time I went
was 'before it happened' - I was horrified by the meticulous care
with which people chose their meat.

Annie Ernaux

Letter Out

Today was hard and strange.
I have no grandparents left. I wore my Mexican sandals
that I love, and I was good to my cousins, who I barely
know. I was even better to my dad's brother who
reminds me of a dimly lit version of him. It was rough
and beautiful, there are lots of bunches of flowers to be
nurtured now. But there's nothing like uncles you've
barely met who tell you – keep the books, you know
were promised to you. Try not to forget, I am not death's
sole initiate and miss my gran who was rude and elegant
and opinionated. But she was 87. And that's reasonable,
and that's time. I've lit a fire. Everyone else is in bed
thinking no thoughts or remembering many things, but
of course I can't leave the fire. I made it big enough so I
wouldn't be able to leave it for hours. I am burning the
cardboard boxes all the pies we had for tea came home
in. The boxes that contained scotch eggs flare and blaze,
red and wonderfully. I have attended death at home
before and still can't believe that childhood is over.
I've learned to cry quite recklessly without the wish for
you to come to me but when I make a fire you make a
fire with me. When the last pie box shrivels to embers,
I stay on, right into total darkness.

SUSTENANCE

Milk is very good,
but it is frightful the way it's getting so late again, yet
I can't help it. That is a general lament.

I am already so poisoned that the body can hardly
understand pure fruit.

The quantity of food I consume at present is insufficient
for the body to mend of its own accord, then there's no
hope, apart from miracles.

You praise so arbitrarily when I've eaten enough; today
I ate a great deal and you reproach me; another time
you praise me just as unfairly.

I like to eat it in the comb;
I suppose it can be had only in the fall, and besides
fine light-coloured combs are very rare.

Why didn't I once try beer in the hospital
Lemonade   It was all so boundless.

Might I try a little ice cream today?

(Kafka, *Conversation Slips*)

•

A little fire —
and streaming out towards Bedgebury forest
the Milky Way.

Where has your life gone so suddenly?

Butterfly Requiem

*

Morning after the funeral
counting butterflies
on summer lilac

for an app which tells me
    I am a citizen scientist.

*

Miss you most in the morning
when everything is still being found
and turned over in the light of dreams.

*

Still cold Buddleia hung with butterflies
their outer wings taut and drawn close
like distrustful horse's ears.

*

Lost count of the opening
and closing wounds
of Painted Ladies.

*

Short-boned wings of my grandmothers back.
Long-boned hands.
They are the sad white bones of parting.

*

Today is like a little girl reading a missing cat poster
pinned to a tree then running to catch her father's hand.

A butterfly
tears itself
from the buddleia.

The fish greet me
teary-eyed.

*

The post came
and after that
just silent sunlight
and oak leaves streaming into the pond.
The world falls off
        like a flower vase.

*You'll have to warn the girl about the glass;
she sometimes comes in barefoot.*
                Kafka, *Conversation Slips*

Her Smile

Far past the point where any fall was trivial,
I never saw her smiling too unlike the first
smile I remember being hers:
      a smile like a sweet pea
      brimming with beautiful water.

For Sally

her best and oldest friend who cried
and cried while bravely reversing
out of Beckenham crematorium,
the cynosure of all caring eyes:

there's nothing to give you,
I simply will always remember.

That time you came when I was kept in bed, how easy it was
                    Kafka, *Conversation Slips*

[Dr Klopstock reports that this refers to the days in Prague after
Kafka's return from Berlin and before going to the Sanatorium. At
that time Kafka noticed the first symptoms of the disease. Klopstock
writes: "During those days he wrote the story 'Josephine the Singer,
or the Mouse Folk,' and one evening when he had finished the last
page of the story he said to me: 'I think I began to investigate that
animal squeaking at the right time. I have just finished a story about
it.' I didn't have the courage to ask him to let me read it. That same
evening he told me that he felt an odd burning in his throat
whenever he drank certain beverages, especially fruit juices, and
said he was worried that his larynx might be affected."]

The Last Thing

she said to me
on FaceTime, on a tiny screen:

"When are you coming home?"

and she looked very tired.

For the first time
something in her voice
suggests that she will die.

A batik of water-flowers
and ripples rose behind her.

Her face said: it has not stopped getting worse.

The ripples unravelled
like gonfalons above her shoulders,
she lay low in her bed like a ship
and seemed a little crushed below them.

How could something so light
and only made of thread be crushing her?

But the freight upon her was invisible to me.
Her leg had swollen and was weeping
in the night like a wild bird at the foot of the bed
and her voice was petrifying

– already destined
no longer to exist, I suppose

it had been
destined always.

Everyone has their one voice
like every child has their childhood.

Now she is a stranger to it, visitant
of her own song – the scordatura
of which was the delight and lumber of herself.

What am I trying to write down?

Her silence is the dreadful
all-powerful theme.

Not long after the service

comes a Sunday
near to nothing.

Having bloodied the weatherboarding
the sunset attacks steeples and pines.

A nesting sob
   tests its wings.

The fight to close the glottis
feels like a lump in the throat.

Memories keep
well in the glottis.

At last, I speak
in the voice of a bewildered child.

Conversely
this prevents us all being struck down
by sudden loneliness.

...let us touch
tender spots tenderly...
Kafka, *letter to Robert Klopstock.*
postmark: February 29, 1924

•

The world is a little soft
and paralysed this morning.

A night of watching
W- try to stand upright in dreams
unsteady as a giraffe on its first day.

I am crossing the steep back of the year
on pale tides, long gliding sleep
the colour of crushed grasshoppers.

Michael Rosen says to sleep
is to make peace
with the landscape of your body.

Long live the cold clouds racing over me.

•

And W- was a daughter too
but there is no sea-canoe
can take me to those bays
and inlets of half-truths,
now my grandmother is dead
there is no one to tell her story
as it really was:

>   what is not remembered
>   shall not be remembered

what was unsafe to tell
has disappeared. With memory
you are *forced to be a good loser*

everything runs away from us
– rivulets that leave no traces.

Final Portrait

The hardening body
becomes its own statue

then shawled in fire, becomes a dust
and the pale birch still strewing seeds.

The day after the day
strange flowers clog the sink

like bright fish at the end
of hairy umbilical stems.

Strangeness and changes. The birch
still seeds like blossom. Where are you now

approaching? The water mill village?
Or somewhere light and truly good

      with a night-time
dark enough to see the stars?

Stars
we wouldn't recognise.

Asleep or awake
the night is long

beneath the Milky Way
that is called the River of Heaven.

Waters of night bathe your eyes and
wet the brick-red powder of blood.

May you be forever and a day
by still, depopulated waters

trailing your fingers through floors of fair weather
with us all a great distance beneath you.

On Loughrigg

I.

Our path
is a watercourse
the pearl-grey colour of pear.

An autumn lake
is drubbing the fells

watering
the ancient Briton
under the hill
under harebell
and bristling restharrow.

What was falling without ending
lifts suddenly away.

Fugitive streams
vanish like snakes
into the moorland,

rain and people rest under the same quilt.

Hidden in the wind
like birdsong on the mountain

we climb
bright emptiness
stepping over lost rivers

their tails and their long cascades
disappear between the terrier's paws

washing unseen fossils on their way
down to where the earth remembers
a time before all flowers.

II.

Out of breath
behind my mum
in sudden rain –
it is her birthday.

Autumn rain
feeling more like the rain of spring.
Truly good rain.

•

I start to say something to W- in my dream
and profound weeping wakes me.
After waking, I weep again.
Nothing remains of the dream
only the crane white hospital bed,
leek white, empty, white as milk
from the broken stem of a dandelion.

DREAMS

Now I have dreamed that R. is at the door and I am to give him a sign that I am somehow ready, but at the same time I knew that you [Dora] were on the terrace and did not want to disturb you by making the sign. Difficult problem.

It was a kind of bargain in half-sleep. I was promised that I would manage to sleep through the din, but that in return I must promise something else. I promised but have forgotten what

(Kafka, *Conversation Slips*)

Suddenly and Strangely

I.

the top layer of my family
has peeled away like dark colours
from the margins of dawn
- I miss the night
sky that used to shelter me.

II.

It seems we lose someone
of extraordinary dearness
every four years

and only one time
in three is it the dog.

III.

Autumn already -
how few folds
to make a year.

Notes on the Kitten

I.

She is dreaming, or hunting
wine-corks in the covers.

When she dreams
it is like she is dancing in a very narrow space
 - something inside her is stubbing its toes
and knocking its head on the underside
                    of her furred edges.
When she plays
it is like she is a child and a bird
of prey: perceiving keenly
that which is ill-hidden:
            the mouse
I have concealed with its tail trailing brightly
from the safety of the sofa leg like a ribbon
                    marking a book.

II.

Sleeping, her ears stay awake.

But the body sleeps deeply
like lichen on a stone

that's crept a million years
just to cling on peacefully

      and stretch
the quiet web of itself.

By her instinctual proclivity
for hunting feathers,

by her natural ability
to eat them whole,

she makes all my race's secrets
inferior.

III.

Fell asleep
under cover of purring
that faded in and out
like a turning lighthouse.

Her whole-body trembles.
Where the tip of her paw touches my arm
the skin of it is trembling too.

IV.

Held up my nameless kitten as an offering
(not her body, but my care for her)
then set her down gently before the gas-fire,
before my father and my grandmother.

Now they have both vanished
I love them much more perfectly,
and *finished, they are endurable
and perfect.*

I kiss the kitten on the top of her head
and tell her it is a kiss and she billows
with purring in the valley of my legs.

V.

At dawn
the kitten looks at me
as if I am part of her dream.

The Turning Year

I.

I guess
   after five years
it has come back to a Saturday

because he died on a Saturday.

G-
my father,

who I cannot see
and cannot turn my mind away from,

how can we have been
   without you for so long?

  After five years
what my heart does not believe
   it believes a little more.

There is no way to know: not this, not anything.

The feast day of our first dead is the 23rd of January

(Bedgebury Forest,
 accident without substance,
     9 centigrade).

My mum plans her feast:

"Steak. Crème fraîche, with peppercorns. Slice
up an onion. That's what G- .. that's what we did.

But I don't think I'll do that
            just for myself
                now."

II.

In my memory
you are using up your life

growing straight into death
like a daylily in the slow attrition of one day.

Your body I remember
as the calmest of dead men

laid out long and useless
like the standing leg of a flamingo.

It's not that I've lost my imagination
but time has slowly robbed me
of even the illusion of closeness to you

my ever-receding horizon.

Your silence confounds me.
That it is continuous
hurts me daily, and
after the pain
        terror.

Maybe you don't remember
the voice of my society
was born from your mouth.

III.

Let today in like a dog that followed us
down the beach and cried

on the stoop of the holiday cottage:
tristesse, blind-trust, sunlight.

One day maybe soon
I will see what has happened now
has happened for good

and walk with it like a dog-not-for-keeping
saying, "We can only be this close.

(Pause)

Thank you."

IV.

See you as a star
falling like it was made for falling.

A star that knows
the path ahead and no road home.

Down here
someone is still
singing the song you sung.

After five years
it has come back
to a Saturday.

My mum says: *I can't believe it's been so long*
and, *I almost feel I've been on my own forever.*

V.

We live on

learning again
what I already knew:
we shall spend the rest of our lives together

eerily or otherwise.
And I remain

in the end a poet.
An unknown one:

no barbarian successes,
    no great sorrows

        but one.

Restrictive feasting.
Bedtime swig
of Cioran:

        to live is to suffer
        the sorcery of the possible

that's almost hopeful, isn't it?

Slept as though utterly safe
under peatbog, dreamless.

It is useless to try to integrate life and death and to behave rationally in the presence of something that is not rational: each must manage as well as they can in the tumult of their feelings. I can understand all last wishes and the total absence of them.

Simone De Beauvoir
A Very Easy Death

The End. Beginning a prolonged struggle.

Dziga Vertov Group
Wind from the East

Appendix
On Kafka's Conversation Slips

Max Brod, Kafka's friend and biographer writes that: "during his final illness [tuberculosis of the larynx] at Sanatorium Wienerwald in Kierling, Kafka was not supposed to speak, an injunction he obeyed most of the time. He communicated with Dora Diamant, Robert Klopstock, and others by scribbling notes on slips of paper. Usually these notes were mere hints; his friends guessed the rest."[1]

Hélène Cixous characterises them beautifully as belonging to "the economy of the dying ... tender and precise: the extraordinary courtesy of a man who has nothing left to live."[2] I have woven some of his slips like ribbons through these pages so that the voiceless may keep each other company and maybe speak together a little. When we are bereaved, we also can feel voiceless and the dead can be very vocal.

[1] *Kafka: Letters to Family, Friends and Editors*, 1977, 419-425pp.
[2] *Three Steps on the Ladder of Writing*, 1990, 151-152pp.

Appendix ii
Kafka's Last Year: *An Epistolary Patchwork*

did not write because I was sick (high temperature, chills, and
fever, and as a postlude to illness a single visit from the doctor for
160 crowns)
did not write because of a slight clouding of the mind,
      caused by digestive disturbances and the like.
You are right to add that reminder of "warm, well-fed Bohemia,"
but it just won't very well do; to some extent I am stuck here

often I've read the article on Musorgski (and still don't know how
to spell the name),
rather like a child who clings to the doorjamb at the entrance to a
ballroom and looks in
      on a grand revel of strangers.
[to Max Brod, Berlin-Steglitz; mid-January 1924]

      There is little
to tell about myself,   a somewhat shadowy life;
anyone who isn't looking squarely at it cannot notice it.
      An acquaintance, a young painter, now has a fine job;
I've envied him for it more than once. He is a street book-peddler.
[Postcard to Robert Klopstock. Berlin-Steglitz; January 26, 1924]

      I may be making a mistake (and being punished in
advance by the exorbitant rent, which as rents go is really not at
all excessive for this apartment but in reality is beyond my means)
by moving into the home of a deceased writer, Dr. Carl Busse (he
died in 1918), who at least during his lifetime would certainly have
detested me.

      But I'm moving in nonetheless;
the world is everywhere full of perils, so let this special one
emerge if it will

from the darkness of all the unknown dangers.
[Postcard to Feliz Weltsch. Berlin Steglitz; January 28, 1924]

in brief: I cannot come, am sick
[to Ludwig Hardt. Berlin-Zehlendorf; start of February, 1924]

Two letters and a postcard I began have long been drifting
around the apartment somewhere.
You will never receive them.
Recently I looked for your letter before last, could
not find it; then it turned up in a Hebrew book I hadn't opened for a
whole month.
[to Robert Klopstock. Berlin-Zehlendorf; February 29, 1924]

Dear Robert, No, no traveling, no such wild adventure;
we'll meet anyhow, without all that, in a quieter manner, more in
keeping with weak bones.

I am resisting a sanatorium, also resisting a boarding-house,
 but what's the use since I cannot resist the fever.

100.4° has become my daily bread.

It is very lovely here to lie on the veranda and watch the
sun working on two tasks, each difficult in its own way:
to awaken me and the birch alongside me to natural life
(the birch seems to be somewhat ahead)

sometimes the thought of peacefully burying myself alive in the
sanatorium is not at all so unpleasant.
And then again it horrifies me when I consider that I shall be losing
freedom even for those few warm months that are predestined for
freedom.

For so many years what an aura of Paris and of literature
surrounded Holitscher and the titles of his novels
    – and now here is this aging man crying
   over the hardships of that whole period.
He was unhappy then,
  but one cannot help thinking:
  If only I had been unhappy that way just once;
  I really should have tried to be unhappy that way.
[to Robert Klopstock. Berlin-Zehlendorf; start of March, 1924]

   Probably the larynx is the chief problem.
Verbally I don't learn anything definite, since in discussing tuberculosis
of the larynx everybody drops
into a shy, evasive, glassy-eyed manner of speech.   all that in
connection with very malignant pain probably suffices. I have no contact
with the rest of the place,
     lie in bed, also can only whisper.

  The place seems to be a great gossipers' nest from balcony to
balcony; for the time being it doesn't bother me.
[Postcard to Robert Klopstock. Sanatorium Wiener Wald; April 7, 1924]

  As for me, it's evidently the larynx
[Postcard to Max Brod. Sanatorium Wiener Wald; April 9, 1924
postcript by Dora Diamant indicates that the patient's condition
is very grave]

  so swollen that I cannot eat;
they must (they say) undertake alcohol injections into the nerve,
probably also surgery.

  I am afraid of your codeine.
[Postcard to Robert Klopstock. Sanatorium Wiener Wald;
* April 13, 1924]*

forgive the epistolary and telegraphic noise that surrounded you
on my account. It was needless, prompted by weak nerves (how
boastfully I speak and yet I've cried without reason several times
today; my neighbour died during the night)

> he sent me the novel (I was frightfully hungry
>   for a suitable book) and roses.
>
[to Max Brod. Vienna; April 20, 1924]

> If you also count in the fact that I am allowed to speak only
in whispers and even that
not too often, you will gladly postpone the visit.

Since I cannot show the visitors – and what is more, such visitors
as you two would be – major, undeniable progress, measurable
even by lay eyes, I think we should rather let it be.

> So shall we not let it ride for the present, dear parents?

You must not think you could do anything to improve or amplify
my treatment here.
[to Julier and Hermann Kafka. Kierling; May 19, 1924]

… it was not an exceptionally bad day; you mustn't think that; it
was just worse than the preceding day; this is the way the time and
the fever goes on.

there are of course a few tiny items of good cheer, but it's
impossible for me to communicate them they shall have to be
reserved for a visit like the one I so wretchedly spoiled. Keep well.
> Thanks for everything.
[Postcard to Max Brod. Kierling; May 20, 1924]